EX LIBRIS

UNIVERSITATIS SANCTI JOANNIS

GROWING UP
MASAI
▼▼▼

TOM SHACHTMAN

GROWING UP MASAI

PHOTOGRAPHS BY DONN RENN

MACMILLAN PUBLISHING CO., INC.

NEW YORK

Macmillan Publishing Co., Inc.
866 Third Avenue, New York, N.Y. 10022
Collier Macmillan Canada, Ltd.
Printed in the United States of America
10 9 8 7 6 5 4 3 2 1

Library of Congress Cataloging in Publication Data
Shachtman, Tom, date.
   Growing up Masai.
   Summary: Describes the daily activities of two
young members of the Masai tribe.
   1. Masai—Juvenile literature. [1. Masai—
Social life and customs] I. Renn, Donn. II. Title.
DT429.S5   967.6′2   80-25017   ISBN 0-02-782550-7

ACKNOWLEDGMENTS

My special thanks to Rajni Desai for his help and kindness; to
Amboseli and Kilimanjaro Safari Lodge; to Patty Purchase and Di;
to Mehmood Quraishy of the Color Center in Nairobi; to Masoud
Quraishy of Kenya Photo Murals; to Suku Shah; to Nagin Rathod for
keeping my Land Rovers moving; to Thorn Tree Safaris and Dennis Lakin;
to E. K. Ruchiami, Office of the President, Kenya; to Z. O. Kongoro
of the Ministry of Tourism and Wildlife of Kenya; to Benjamin
Kamar, Chief of Turkana, Lodwar; to Wilson Musa Wambua; to Alexander,
my interpreter; and, of course, to all the children of the Masai—

                                                          —D. R.

TO OUR CHILDREN

T.S. and D.R.

The rain falls in a rhythmic beat on the roof of the *boma*. Close by, the cattle and goats can be heard moving about restlessly, and in the distance, there is the roar of a lion. It is still dark, before the dawn, near the day of changing for the moon. Lekorrio and his sister Namaiyiai crawl from their grass beds on all fours through the opening which leads to the outside. The cattle manure is cold, and the children's bare feet make a squishing sound as they move through it.

It is *Oloirurujuruj*, the drizzling season after the long rains, and it is still wet most of the time. The children can barely see Kilimanjaro, the White Mountain, where *Ruwa* the sun god lives. This year, the rainy season came early to the savanna, just as the tribal elders said it would. The elders know everything about the world. They know the legends, how the Masai began, where the sacred cattle came from, when to hold the ceremonies and celebrations.

Last night, father Lekeni was in the boma with mother Muriet. The children go up to him and bow, for they must show all elders great respect. They may not speak until he has touched them on the head. Father Lekeni has two other wives and many more children, some of whom live in other bomas in this *manyatta*.

Everyone who is awake sniffs the air, trying to learn the weather of the day. All hope that it will soon be the time of *Kujorok*, when the whole countryside is as green and hairy as a caterpillar, and there is good grazing.

Out on the savanna near the manyatta, grass eaters such as gazelles, wildebeests, and zebras gather at water holes. They spend most of their days grazing peacefully. There are also lions, cheetahs, baboons, giraffes, and water buffaloes on the savanna. Lekorrio and Namaiyiai see rhinoceroses and elephants every day.

One of the stories the elders tell relates that it was an angry elephant who pulled the rhinoceros's horn into such a funny position on top of his head. There is a Masai game with rhinos: You must find a sleeping rhino and take turns putting small rocks on his back. Whoever puts on the last rock before the rhino wakes up has won the game. It is very dangerous.

Of all the animals, the Masai have the most respect for the lion. These big predators usually eat the grass eaters. Lions do not have to kill every day—one big catch may last several days, if the lions can keep it away from the hyenas. Occasionally, when it is very dry and the hunting is bad, a lion will try to kill a Masai cow or goat for food. The Masai must guard against this.

Lions are also important to the Masai because the *moran*, the male warriors, must prove their courage by killing a lion with a spear. It takes a team of five of the warriors to do this, and a lot of practice. It doesn't happen very often.

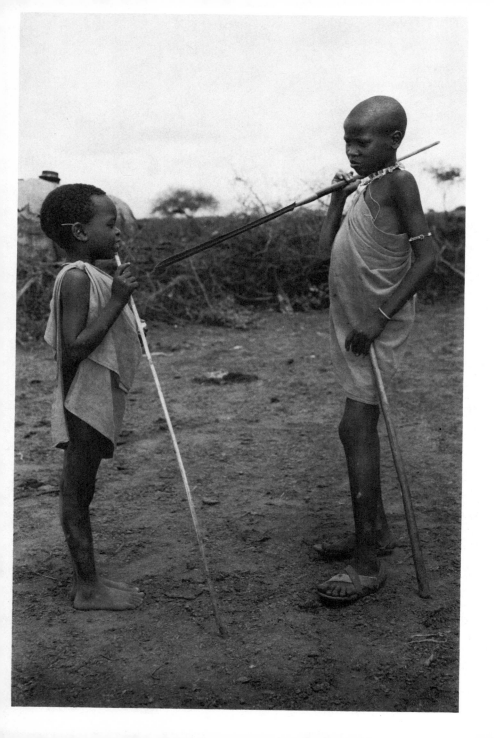

Lekorrio hopes when he grows up he will be a very fierce moran. He practices throwing his spear and watches the older ones to learn. The moran spend much time grooming themselves—painting their bodies and doing up their hair with red ocher—so they will appear fierce and scare their enemies. Although the moran are the warriors of the Masai, they are not the only leaders. The elders have more knowledge and more responsibility.

In the past, the Masai made many wars. If a neighboring tribe stole cattle, or made off with some women, or took slaves, a band of moran would gather. They would make themselves fierce, travel at night, and surprise their enemies, bringing back the cattle. They would even take some captives to replenish the tribe, or make trophies. The Masai have a great reputation for strength and cunning. Lekorrio is proud that people fear the Masai. But today there is not much fighting. Occasionally, a band of moran will go out and steal a bull for a feast, but it is all in fun.

The day's work has already begun. Before the cattle can leave the thorn-bush enclosure, mother Muriet, sister Namaiyiai, and the other women and girls milk them. This is women's work. Men never milk the animals. This is just the way things are. As the elders say, "A zebra takes its stripes wherever it goes."

The men check the cattle for diseases. Cattle have more problems than they have flies! The men know all there is to know about the animals; a man's wealth is measured by the number of his cattle.

For Lekorrio and other *layoni*, the day's work really starts as they herd their fathers' animals out of the thornbush gates toward the day's grazing area. Often, the family dogs accompany the boys and the cattle. Lekorrio knows each of father Lekeni's animals by sight. He can tell at a glance if one of them is missing, though he would never count them, for to do so would bring bad luck.

The grazing area for today is several hours walk out from the manyatta. Masai are famous walkers and runners and have exceptionally long legs and arms. Lekorrio walks for a long time with the cattle and never sees people from any other manyattas. But he always stays within sight of Kilimanjaro, for that is the center of Masai country.

Out on the grazing ground far away from his parents, on guard against lions and cattle stealers, Lekorrio feels he has a very responsible task. There are no warriors to protect the cattle. He must do it himself. Here in his charge is not only father's wealth but also the food for the tribe. He must be an expert in everything about the animals. Often a calf or a kid may be born, and he must help the mother animal give birth.

The sun gets very hot near midday, and there is little shade to be found anywhere. Herding is a hard job, but all the layoni do it.

The layoni talk about the upcoming advancement ceremony. People will gather from many manyattas, and Lekorrio's age-group will move up a step toward the time when they will become moran. At the ceremony, Lekorrio and his friends will kindle the fire for their younger brothers, just as some older boys will kindle the fire for them. Every boy is linked in this way to those older and younger than himself. It is a bond of friendship that lasts all through life. It's hard for Lekorrio to wait until the special year when he becomes a moran, but as the elders say, "You cannot wave an arrow before it is thrown." You have to learn to be patient.

Namaiyiai and the other *ndito* stay around the manyatta. After the milk has been taken from the cows, it must be divided into three batches. The first is for drinking fresh, the second is for storing in gourds in which it will turn sour and solid, and the third is for mixing with blood for a special Masai drink. Namaiyiai must also clean gourds with cattle urine as part of her daily work. Then she picks parasites off the young animals.

While they are working, the ndito sometimes tell each other riddles handed down from the elders. Here is one: Can you name four great wonders? They are a stool, a calabash, a snake, and water. Why are they wonders? Because a stool has legs and yet does not walk; a calabash has milk and does not drink it; a snake moves even though it has no legs; and water moves even though it, too, has no legs.

The women and girls also keep the boma in good condition. A boma is built with twigs, which are shaped into a dome. The framework is covered with grass or branches of leaves, and then plastered with a thick layer of fresh cow dung. The ndito collect the dung from the middle of the manyatta, where the cattle spend the night. They use it to patch up the huts. During the time of *Nkokua*, the long rains, when the constellation of the Plough was seen in the sky every night, the boma needed repair every day. Sometimes, if the land is too dry, or the cattle have come down with a disease, or if an elder has foreseen that the family should move, the entire family picks up and travels to another boma many hours walk away. The family has several other bomas in different manyattas. Wherever the family goes, the women fix up the bomas. In half a day, a woman can make an old home into a new one.

When she is not repairing the boma, or cleaning it, or caring for her little brother, or helping her mother with any tasks, Namaiyiai still has more chores to do. With the other ndito, she must collect firewood for the cooking fires and also get water for eating and washing.

Namaiyiai looks forward to the time when her age-group becomes eligible for marriage. Although her body has not yet changed into a woman's, the time for marriage is only a few years away. Many of the ndito have had marriages arranged for them by their fathers, with men in distant manyattas. Father Lekeni promised Namaiyiai to a man even before she was born! She wonders what he will look like. Namaiyiai hopes he will be a warrior, not an elder, and she hopes she will have the honor of being his first wife.

When moran are old enough and have proven themselves worthy, they can become elders. Women, once they have borne four healthy children, can also become elders. Having four healthy children is not an easy task. Many children die before they have even been named. It is sad, but the will of the gods cannot be changed. As mother Muriet says, "A holed calabash cannot be filled."

This afternoon, the elders have decided the moran should take some blood from a cow to mix with milk for a special meal. The moran have to use a special arrow so it will not go to far into the throat vein. After the animal is bled, it will not be cut again for months.

The sun is sinking in the sky. Lekorrio starts home with the animals. Before the evening meal, the thorn-bush enclosure must be closed behind the animals, so that during the night no lions can attack.

While the women prepare food, layoni may practice throwing spears at targets, and ndito may work at beads for necklaces and long earrings. The moran and older girls may learn dances or groom themselves.

At the meal, the elders are served first, the children last. Occasionally the Masai will eat meat broiled over the fire. Most of the time everyone drinks milk and eats some herbs and other plants. At feasts and other ceremonies, there is beer made from fermented honey. A special bird called a honey-bird leads the Masai to a tree where the bees have made a nest; when they knock down the tree and get the honey, there is always some left for the bird. And honey is one of the children's favorite foods.

When it is dark, there is singing and stories. The elders tell many legends. Here is one: The bee, the fly, and the dog were arguing about which animal owns the Masai. The fly said that because he went everywhere with the Masai and the cattle, it was he who was the owner. The dog disagreed, saying he also went everywhere with the Masai, and furthermore, he always warned of danger—so it was *he* who owned the Masai.

The bee was the last to speak. He said he was related to the maggot in the cow's dung, and therefore was very close to the Masai and to the cow. Also, said the bee, he had to collect nectar and had to fight battles to protect his honey so that the Masai could come along and get it. When he threw his one arrow—his stinger—the bee would die. This is what he did for the Masai. And the honey that the bee gave was used for making beer. Without honey beer, there would be no marriage ceremony, and that would mean there would be no more Masai children at all! That is why the Masai, the legend says, really belong to the bee.

Around the fire, in the dark evening, the Masai are all together, talking of the ways of the earth and the sky, of the hard work that is always to be done, of the rewards of living in the savanna. Friendship is a great joy. People are always more worthwhile than animals. "Happiness is as good as food," says a Masai proverb.

Lekorrio and Namaiyiai sing of becoming warriors and maidens, of having great herds of cattle, of getting married and raising many beautiful children. "Life cannot be hurried," the elders say, but they also say "daylight follows a dark night." Tomorrow, the sun will come up near Kilimanjaro, and soon after, the drizzling will be gone, and the days hot, the earth filled with good grass. The little black-and-white birds which feed in the midst of the cattle will appear, and then it will be time for the ceremony of the new year. ▼▼▼▼▼▼▼▼

AFTERWORD

The Masai are a group of tribes that live on the rolling high plains of East Africa, near the equator. They inhabit parts of the countries of Kenya and Tanzania. Their way of living has existed without much change for about a thousand years.

Today, many Masai have the opportunity to leave their ancient way of life and go to towns where they can become educated in more modern ways. They can live in buildings not made out of cow dung; they can learn to read and write; they can get jobs, earn money, watch television, travel to different places, and have good medical care. Some Masai do go to the cities. Some have become Olympic running champions. Others are doctors or farmers or businessmen. But most Masai do not go to the towns. They prefer to live on the savanna in their ancient style of existence, because they feel that if they were to become "civilized," they would stop being like their brothers and sisters. They don't want to change. They want to be Masai.

GLOSSARY

boma—a mud hut

Kilimanjaro—the huge mountain on the border between
Kenya and Tanzania

Kujurok—the sixth month of the Masai year

layoni—a young boy

manyatta—a Masai village; a group of huts

moran—a male Masai warrior

ndito—a young girl

Nkokua—the season of the long rains; also, the little
cluster of stars known as the Plough

Oloirurujuruj—the drizzling season after the long rains

Ruwa—a name for the sun god

savanna—grassy plains with scattered trees, such as the
high plains near Kilimanjaro